BELIEVE IN YOURSELF
A KEY TO LIFE GUIDED JOURNAL

Cover and text art and design by Lesley Ehlers
Cover Illustration in diecut by Jo Gershman

The guided text in this journal is excerpted from
The Key to Life by Sophia Bedford-Pierce
Copyright © 1995 Peter Pauper Press, Inc.
and *Believe in Yourself: A Woman's Journey*
by Beth Mende Conny
Copyright ©1994, 1996 by Peter Pauper Press, Inc.

Visit us at
www.peterpauper.com

$\mathcal{L}$ife is a book and you are its author. Believing in your own intuition and instincts is key. Asking yourself new and empowering questions and writing your thoughts and observations will allow you the freedom to take both small steps and great strides. There is not one way to accomplish this. There is not one name for happiness, contentment, or caring. Let the words that you write here serve as your own key to life.

The greatest
revenge is to
accomplish
what others
say you
cannot do.

Don't regret
what might
have been.
Accept what
is and rejoice
in what is yet
to be.

Don't wait
for your
world to
change.
Change it
yourself.

Live today
fully and
you create a
lifetime of
meaningful
memories.

There are no
impossible
dreams, just
our limited
perception
of what is
possible.

It is
in the
company
of a good
friend
that the
heart
finds
a home.

The
only true
failure
is the
person
who fails
to try.

We cannot
predict the
inevitable.
We can only
accept it
as our life
unfolds.

Potential
is not
something
you have to
live up to,
but it is
something
you must
use.

To have a
satisfying
relationship
with your
family,
friends, and
colleagues,
you must
first have
a satisfying
relationship
with
yourself.

You may be
disappointed
if you fail,
but you are
certain to be
disappointed
if you
never try.

Embrace
change,
and you've
made a
friend for
life.

Only with
understanding
can you
truly
celebrate
your life.

Do great
things in
your life,
but do
small things
as well.

There's
nothing
wrong
with being
realistic—
as long
as you
create your
own reality.

Don't
strive to be
better than
others;
strive to
be better
than your
best self.

Taking
charge of
your life
takes time—
and a bit
of faith and
courage.

Embrace
love. The
light it
brings can
illuminate
your
feelings.

The words
you choose
to tell the
truth are as
important
as the
decision to
be truthful.

The key to
happiness
will never
become
apparent if
you have not
previously
considered
that
happiness
is worth
having.

Strength is
measured by
restraint.

Making life
less difficult
for others
is to be
encouraged.
Creating
happiness
for others
is to be
rewarded.

If you
measure
your value
by who you
are, there
is no end
to your
reserves.

When
you
overcome
loss you
gain new
strength.

If you can
see the
beauty of
what you
aspire to,
it doesn't
matter if
you achieve
it all.
Simply to
aspire is
no mean
achievement.

Knowledge
can be
captured by
the mind;
faith must be
apprehended
by the soul.

The key
to life
unlocks
beauty in
all things.